Creative DECORATIVE PAINTING

A J.B. Fairfax Press Publication

EDITORIAL
Managing Editor: Judy Poulos
Editorial Assistant: Ella Martin
Editorial Coordinator: Margaret Kelly

PHOTOGRAPHY
Steve Tanner, Di Lewis, Andrew Elton

ILLUSTRATIONS
Margaret Metcalfe

DESIGN AND PRODUCTION
Manager: Sheridan Carter
Layout: Gavin Murrell
Finished Art: Steve Joseph

Published by J.B. Fairfax Press Pty Limited
80-82 McLachlan Avenue
Rushcutters Bay 2011 Australia
A.C.N. 003 738 430

Formatted by J.B. Fairfax Press Pty Limited
Printed by Toppan Printing Co,
Hong Kong

JBFP 154
CREATIVE DECORATIVE PAINTING
ISBN 1 86343 105 5

DISTRIBUTION AND SALES
Newsagents Direct Distributors
150 Bourke Road, Alexandria NSW 2015
Tel: (02) 353 9911 Fax: (02) 669 2305

Sales Enquiries:
J.B. Fairfax Press Pty Limited
Tel: (02) 361 6366 Fax: (02) 360 6262

Contents

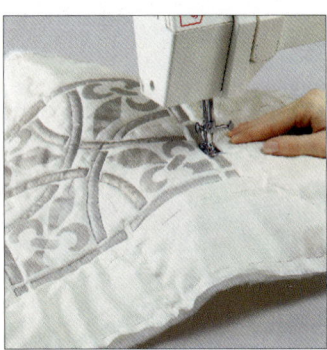

42 Furniture Facelifts

Transform your home with these decorative painting and stencilling projects for every room.

Decorative Painting

Somewhere deep inside all of us is an artist just waiting for the opportunity to shine. In the past this has remained an unrealised ambition for most people. These days, thanks to the arrival of easy-to-use, almost foolproof, paints and the revival of traditional decorative techniques, anyone can be an artist.

Just as exciting is the discovery that you can use an enormous variety of objects and surfaces for your canvas. You can transform just about anything with some paint and a little imagination. Craft shops sell an increasing variety of objects specifically for this purpose, such as lidded balsa wood boxes, plain china, craft paper lampshades, picture frames and wooden items of various kinds. If you are un-sure of where to find these items, check the advertisements in your favourite craft magazine. Remember, too, that decorative painting techniques will do wonders for that much-used treasure stored in the garage.

In this book, you will find a host of easy-to-do projects that cover painting on glass, fabric, plaster, wood and ceramics. The full-sized templates for the designs are on the pattern sheet, ready for you to trace off. You don't need to have any special skills – if you can trace a design and hold a paintbrush, you can achieve anything in this book.

CHOOSING YOUR DESIGN

If you are a novice, you will probably feel more comfortable using a template exactly as it is given. As you gain confidence and skill, experiment with the designs, changing elements or colours until you find an arrangement that pleases you. Sources of inspiration are all around you. As well as books, look out for tile and fabric patterns, china designs, gift-wrapping paper, ceramic tiles and wallpaper patterns.

Once you have chosen your design, you may find that it is not the size you need. The simplest way to enlarge or reduce a design is with a photocopier. If this is not possible, you will need to use the grid method which is described on page 7.

TRANSFERRING THE DESIGN

Some designs can be transferred quite easily to the object you are painting – particularly so when an irregular, freehand look is called for or if the design is very simple.

If you have a more complex design where some exactness is required, there is a method to help you. First, trace the design from the pattern sheet on to a piece of tracing paper. Next, place the tracing over the area it is to occupy and tape it in place with masking tape. Slip a piece of graphite paper (such as Transitrace) between the tracing and the surface and go over the lines with a sharp pencil or stylus. This will transfer the outline to the surface with lines of graphite which you can erase when the painting is complete. These graphite papers come in a light and a dark form so you can choose one that is appropriate to the surface you are painting on.

MATERIALS

These days there is an enormous variety of paint and paint-type products on the market. For best results, you should always choose a product that is specifically formulated for the surface you are working on. Some products are multi-purpose and are therefore particularly useful to have in your collection.

Always try to buy the best brushes you can afford and look after them. Clean your brushes after every use – in mineral turpentine (for solvent-based paints) or water (for water-based paints). For more tips on looking after your brushes, see page 9.

You will need a variety of paintbrush sizes, from narrow liner brushes to quite large flat brushes, depending on the projects you choose. Begin with the brushes you need for your first project, then add to your collection as you go.

CHOOSING PAINTS
Acrylic Paints
The easiest paints to use, acrylic paints, are available in a huge range of colours and sizes of containers (from tubes to large cans). Because they are water-based, clean-up is simple. Take care to attend to

this quickly, because once the paint has dried, it will be as permanent as any solvent-based paint and will certainly ruin your brushes.

Acrylic paints can be applied to almost any surface and do not need primer or undercoat. They are equally suitable for indoor or outdoor use and are fully water-proof when dry.

Ceramic Paints

Ceramic paints should be used for items which are largely decorative. Available in a wide range of colours, they give a shiny finish to ceramics, glass, metal and even wood.

Above: Tiles, wrapping paper, fabric, books and china can all provide a rich source of painting designs

They can be coated with a ceramic varnish to give an even glossier and somewhat more durable surface. Do not put items painted with these paints in the dishwasher; wash them carefully by hand in warm soapy water.

Fabric Paints

There are a number of types of fabric paints available today and most are easy to apply. Read the manufacturer's information on the tube, pot or pen to find the one that is suitable for your purpose. Most fabric paints work best when applied to a white or cream surface but some will colour a darker surface quite well. The range of colours is excellent and includes metallic shades as well.

Fabric pens are a very easy option if you want a little more control of the colour, such as outlining or writing. Take care to tape your fabric down when using pens or straight-from-the-tube paints as the fabric can become wrinkled, making it difficult for you to work.

When considering fabric painting, check out the 'puff' type paints and dimensional paints as well; they can give unusual highlights to your work.

Painting on silk requires a slightly different technique. It is crucial to use a frame when painting silk, in order to hold the silk firm and to keep it off the work surface. Special frames are available for this purpose or you can make your own, and special silk pins are used for fastening the silk to the frame. Once the silk is stretched quite tightly in the frame, tape the tracing of your design under the silk and trace over all the outlines with gutta, a gum-like substance. The gutta acts as a barrier, preventing the paint from spreading to an area where it is not wanted. The silk paints (or dyes) flow on to the silk and will flow through any breaks in the gutta. Make sure the gutta lines are continuous and any outlines are closed. Leave the gutta to dry for at least an hour before you begin applying the paint.

Once the paints are dry, the fabrics should be heat-set to make the paint permanent. There are a number of ways you can do this, including steaming, pressing with a warm iron, using your hairdryer, chemical solutions and even microwaving. Follow the manufacturer's instructions and choose the right method for the paints you have used.

Glass Paints

Ideal for decorative items, glass paints give the lovely effect of stained glass. Either solvent- or water-based, they should be applied carefully with a soft clean brush and left to dry for at least a day in a dust-free place. Because the paints do not flow as easily as some others do, a little practice is required to master their use. To achieve a strong deep colour, you may need to apply two coats

Before you begin painting the glass, wash it in warm soapy water, rinse, then dry it thoroughly. To remove any dust or adhering particles, wipe the glass with methylated spirits.

You can use glass paints to decorate china and ceramics but they are not suitable for items which need to cope with a lot of wear and tear. Do not put painted glass in the dishwasher; wash it by hand in lukewarm soapy water.

Other Paints

In addition to these general groups of paint products, there are other products that are quite suitable, such as felt pens. These are very inexpensive and easy to use on a variety of surfaces, such as paper, wood and plaster.

Stencilling paints or crayons are formulated specially to use with stencil brushes in the dabbing or pouncing motion that is required for stencilling. (See page 9 for more on stencilling paints.)

Varnish

Once you have completed your painting, you will need to decide whether to add a coat of varnish and, if you do, whether it should be matt or glossy. The choices are up to you but, generally, a coat of varnish is helpful in giving an extra layer of protection. Make sure your paints are completely dry before you varnish and that the product you use is compatible with the paints and surface it is covering.

Left: Tracing a design off a piece of fabric
Above: Drawing a stencil design from a tracing, leaving 'bridges' in place

STENCILLING

W elcome to the world of stencilling – one of the simplest and most satisfying ways of decorating with paint. Anyone can be a skilful stencil artist, even without the usual talents we associate with the term 'artist'. This book is like a stencil supermarket for the enthusiast. We provide you with a number of wonderful stencil designs – all you have to do is trace them and then cut out your stencil, following the detailed instructions for making stencils on the following pages.

Stencilling is a means of transferring a design, usually a regularly repeating design, to a surface, by applying paint through holes that have been cut out for that purpose. In fact, anything with holes in it, like a piece of lace or a doily, can function as a stencil.

The paints that are used are naturally dictated by the surface to be stencilled. The surface can be made of just about anything – plaster, fabric, wood, china, paper and more.

While stencilling is a very traditional means of decorating, the technique works just as well in a modern setting where it can add considerable warmth and character to an otherwise fairly sterile room*.

The process is not difficult to master. First decide on the motif for your stencil design. Look around and you will find you are surrounded by potential stencil designs – on your favourite china cup, the material of a dress, a book, or a wallpaper pattern. You could even design your own pattern for a stencil. Many people simplify matters even further by painting a ready-to-use stencil. These are becoming more and more popular and are available at quite reasonable cost from craft shops.

Using a popular stencil does not mean that your work will look the same as that of someone else who has used the same stencil. Each person adds their own unique mark, in the colours they choose, the way in which they apply the paint and where they place the stencil.

You can stencil just about anything, but if you are a beginner, choose something small for your first project. Finishing that, and basking in the admiration of family and friends, will encourage you to continue, and to become more adventurous with each project.

*See a stencilled room on page 50

HOW TO STENCIL

Tracing the design

First choose your stencil design. This can be a motif from a book, a piece of fabric or wallpaper, gift wrapping paper, or your own imagination.

If the design needs to be reduced or enlarged, the simplest method is to use a photocopier. If you do not have access to a photocopier, you will have to use the grid method. To do this, draw up a squared grid over the design. Draw another grid with the same number of squares on a fresh sheet of paper. If you want to enlarge the design, make these squares larger than those in the first grid. For example, if you want to double the size of the design, make the squares on the second grid twice the size of the first one. If you want to reduce the size, make the second grid smaller. Now, draw into each square of the second grid, the contents of that square on the first grid, matching the points where outlines cross the grid lines. Don't try to draw in the details until all the main outlines are drawn. Continue in this way until you have transferred the entire design to the new grid.

Making the stencil

If the design is to be used just as it is, with no changes to size or elements of the design, and if you are using clear acetate for your stencil, then it can be traced straight on to the acetate. To make a stencil, trace in the outlines of the elements adding small 'bridges' so that colour areas are enclosed by a continuous line.

For a multi-coloured design, you will find it easier to work if you make a separate stencil for each colour. Trace the entire design on to each stencil, using solid lines for all the parts in one colour and dotted lines for the other outlines. These dotted lines will serve as registration marks for matching up the stencils. For a repeating design, such as a wall pattern or border, add some registration marks, or the dotted outline of the next element at the edges of the design, as well.

Cut out the areas of the design that are to be painted, with a scalpel or sharp craft knife. A self-healing rubber mat will hold the stencil material in place while you work. To ensure accurate cutting, use only the tip of the knife, moving it towards you. Begin cutting in the centre of a space and work towards the edges, turning the acetate rather than the scalpel to cut around curves.

Painting the stencil

Mark with a pencil any guidelines on the surface to be stencilled, such as the true vertical or the distance from a given edge. If the stencil is a repeating design, such as a border, mark in the position of each repeat of the design so that you can make any adjustments to the spacing.

To ensure a clean outline, the stencil must sit flush with the surface to be painted and be held there firmly. Tape the first stencil at its first position with low-tack masking tape.

Choose a paint that is appropriate to the surface to be stencilled. Pour a little of the paint on to an old plate or saucer – stencilling works best when the paint is used quite sparingly. Dip only the ends of the bristles of the stencil brush in the paint, then wipe off any excess paint on to a piece of kitchen paper.

Apply small amounts of paint with a dabbing or pouncing motion. Make sure that you use enough paint to make a clear outline at the edges, but vary the depth of paint across the stencil to give an interestingly shaded effect. Don't use the paint too thickly.

The best fabric for stencilling is a close-woven natural one, such as cotton or silk. Wash and iron the fabric before pinning it out on a work surface that has been protected with sheets of absorbent paper.

When you have large areas to cover and are looking for a soft mottled effect, stencil with a sponge. Always dampen the sponge first before picking up a little paint from the palette. Remove any excess paint on to kitchen paper before you apply the paint with a light dabbing motion.

Clean your equipment with either water or a solvent, depending on the type of paint you have used. It is also very important to clean your stencil often as you work – paint build-up can distort the outlines and even block small holes.

MATERIALS

Tracing Paper and Pencil

Ideally, you will be able to trace your stencil design on to the actual stencil material, but there will be occasions when an intermediate step is required and it is then that you will need tracing paper and pencil. If you are going to adjust the design or isolate a part

of it, you should trace it first on to tracing paper, then make whatever changes you wish before making your stencil.

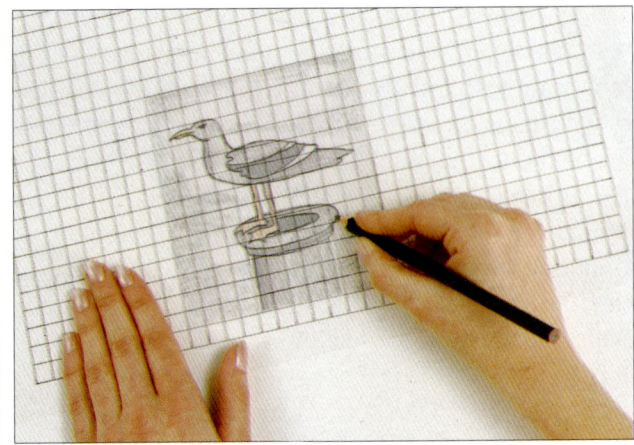

To enlarge a motif, first trace it onto a grid

The Stencil

For a long time, stencils have been made using thick manilla card coated with a 1:1 mixture of mineral turpentine and boiled linseed oil. The treated sheets of card are hung to dry and the excess coating carefully wiped off before use. The sheets are inexpensive and easy to work with, but they have the disadvantage of being opaque so you can't match up design elements or 'see where you are going'.

These days, clear plastic or acetate on rolls or sheets is often used for making stencils instead of manilla card. Choose an acetate that is thick enough to stand up to the wear and tear but not so thick that it is difficult to cut. Because these materials are transparent, they eliminate the need for tracing the design on to tracing paper and then transferring it to the stencil material. You can trace the design directly on to the acetate with a fineline permanent marker pen.

Sharp Craft Knife

Once the design is traced on to the acetate, you will need to cut out those areas that will be covered by paint. Scissors are not suitable; you will need a sharp craft knife or scalpel (available from craft shops).

Cutting Mat

A self-healing rubber mat for cutting on is quite useful but not essential. If you will be using one frequently, it is probably quite a good investment, as the rubber surface not only protects your work surface but your blades as well. The mats are printed with grid lines which are useful for drawing and cutting straight lines.

Masking Tape

A roll of masking tape in two or three widths is a must for stencilling. You will need tape for holding tracings in place, for securing stencils, and for masking surfaces that you wish to protect from paint. The tape is also very useful for running repairs to torn or damaged stencils – much easier than making a new one.

It is possible to buy low-tack masking tape which can be removed without damaging the painted surface. Whether you use low-tack masking tape or the ordinary variety, always exercise great care when pulling the tape away from the surface.

Stencil Brushes

Stencilling requires special brushes that are quite different from ordinary paintbrushes in that the bristle end is flat rather than pointed. This shape is dictated by the way in which stencils are painted – with a dabbing or 'pouncing' motion rather than by stroking.

Always choose the best brushes you can afford and look after them well. Clean them after every use (either in water or solvent – depending on the paint used). If you clean them in solvent, wash them afterwards in a mild detergent solution and dry the bristles with kitchen paper. Never leave paint on the brushes and never store them soaking in water or solvent. Once they are clean and dry, store them standing, with bristles up, in a jar or similar container.

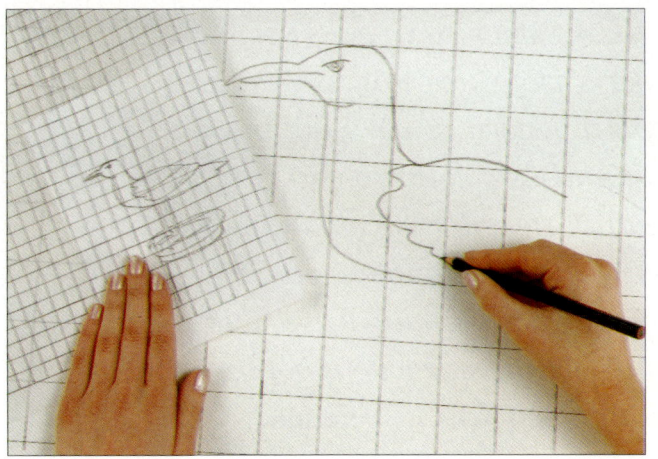

Enlarging the motif by copying it on to a larger grid

Sponges

Natural sponges are very useful for stencilling where the design is quite open and where a soft-textured appearance is desired. Clean your sponges in the same way as the brushes and, when dry, store them in a suitable container.

Paints

You can use just about any paint for stencilling; your choice will usually depend on the surface. There are paints available which are specially made for stencilling. They have the advantage of being fast-drying, allowing you to paint, remove the stencil and replace it in its next position more quickly than you can with most other paints. Stencil paints come in a wide range of colours and can also be mixed to create any colour you wish.

For stencilling on fabric, you can choose from a wide range of paint. Some have the consistency of a thick liquid, others are in powder form, and others are applied directly from a bottle. To allow the item to be washed, the paint needs to be made permanent by fixing with heat. Follow the manufacturer's instructions to heat-set the particular paint you have used.

Special ceramic paints are available for use on tiles, china, ornaments and glass. While these paints are technically permanent, you will need to treat the stencilled object with a little care.

Many other paints can be used for stencilling, including ordinary house paints (either water or oil-based). Cans of spray paint, made for motor vehicles, are very simple to use where a quick overall effect is required on walls, metal surfaces or plastics. If you do choose spray paints, take extra care to mask off the surrounding area with drop-cloths or newspaper before you begin; the spray can travel a surprising distance.

Artists acrylic colours make great stencil paints, particularly for surfaces which need to be flexible.

Ruler

A long plastic ruler is very useful to mark straight lines for placement of the design or for drawing in registration marks for matching up stencils.

Fabric Painting

Painting on fabric is not a modern fad – it has been known since ancient times. These days, with the variety of paints and fabrics available, the possibilities for fabric painting are limitless. Painting your own fabric is a wonderful way of stamping your individuality on your environment.

The most common way to use fabric painting is to decorate a piece of fabric, which is then made up in the usual way into a garment or item of soft furnishing. The other method is to take an existing garment or piece of soft furnishing and then paint a design or motif on it.

Choose paints that are suitable to the project you have in mind, taking into account such factors as wearability and washability. Most fabric paints must be set or 'fixed' with heat to make them permanent and washable.

The delightful tea cloth opposite has been stencilled in a design that mirrors the china pattern. To make a cloth like this, isolate an element or two of your favourite china pattern. It need not be an exact copy but should be harmonious and the colours should match as closely as possible. In this case, separate stencils were made for the border pattern and the corner motif. These were then stencilled around the cloth and napkins as shown. When the paint was dry, the cloth and napkins were pressed on the wrong side with a hot iron to fix the paints, following the manufacturer's instructions.

When you are planning your cloth, take note of which parts of the cloth will be visible when it is laid on the table. Don't waste your efforts on those parts which will not be seen.

PAINTED SILK SCARF

Silk painting, which is much easier than it looks, is not only a very satisfying hobby but also a wonderful source of presents for friends and family.

Left: Tracing the design
Above: The completed scarf

MATERIALS
tracing paper and pencil
90 cm square or 30 cm x 120 cm of
   plain silk (Habutai no. 8)
silk frame
silk pins
masking tape
clear gutta
silk paints
soft paintbrush

INSTRUCTIONS
See the design on the Pull Out
Pattern Sheet.

1 Enlarge the design from the
Pattern Sheet to the required size to
cover your piece of silk. If you do not
have access to a photocopier to enlarge
the design, use the grid method (see
page 7).

2 Stretch the length of silk over the
frame, using special silk pins.
Frames suitable for this purpose are
available from craft shops, ready for you
to assemble. A frame is essential for silk
painting as it keeps the silk quite taut
and raised off the work surface.

3 Tape the design to the frame underneath the silk so that you can see it clearly through the fabric. Trace in the main outlines with the pencil.

4 Follow the pencil lines with the gutta (a gum-like material which serves to separate areas of colour, preventing one colour from bleeding into another). For the gutta to be effective the lines must be continuous; any gaps will allow the silk paint to seep through. Allow the gutta to dry for an hour before beginning to paint.

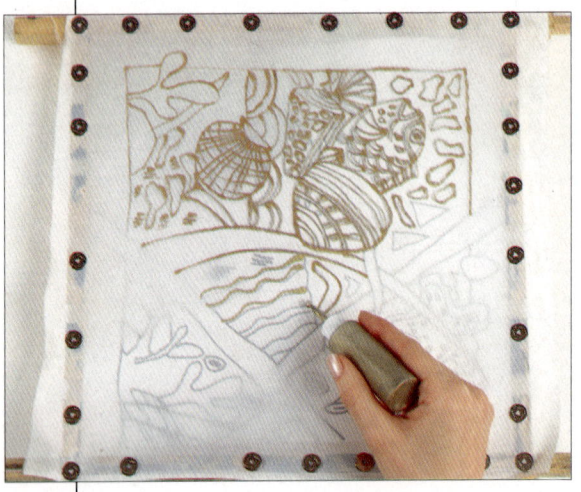

5 Apply the paints with a soft brush, applying the colour between the lines of gutta and letting the paint creep up to the lines. Clean the brush in water before dipping it in the next colour.

6 When the painting is complete and the paint is dry, you can fix the colours by one of the following methods: iron on the back of the silk, steam the silk in a pressure cooker or professional steamer, or use a combination of microwave and fixative. Be guided by the instructions on the paint bottles. Your scarf is now ready to hem.

Top left: Pinning the silk to the frame
Centre left: Outlining the design with the gutta
Left: Painting the design

*Quilted silk cushions
(see page 16)*

QUILTED SILK CUSHIONS

These elegant cream silk cushions have been stencilled with metallic fabric paints and then quilted for a really luxurious effect.

MATERIALS

48 cm square of cream silk for the cushion front
2 pieces of cream silk, each 25 cm x 48 cm, for the cushion back
brown wrapping paper
masking tape
sheets of clear acetate for the stencils
sharp craft knife
cutting board (optional)
fineline permanent marker pen
stencil brush
metallic fabric paints
old saucer or plate for a palette
48 cm square of polyester wadding
cream sewing thread
25 cm zipper
30 cm cushion insert

INSTRUCTIONS

See the design on the Pull Out Pattern Sheet.
1.5 cm seams allowed.

1 Fold the silk square into halves and then into quarters. Press in the creases.

2 Trace the stencil design from the Pattern Sheet on to the acetate with the fineline pen, marking in the horizontal and vertical lines on the design. These indicate the centre of the complete design.

3 Cut out the areas to be painted with the craft knife.

4 Tape the silk square on to the work surface (which has been protected with layers of the brown wrapping paper). Position the stencil on the silk square, matching the pressed lines with the drawn lines on the stencil. Tape the stencil in place on the silk square.

5 Place a small amount of the metallic fabric paint on the saucer or plate. Load the stencil brush with a small amount of paint and, with a dabbing motion, begin to colour in the stencil. Allow the paint to dry before lifting the stencil.

6 Reposition the stencil around the silk square, each time lining up the lines with the creases and allowing the paint to dry before moving on to the next position. When all the painting is complete, leave to dry for twenty-four hours, then set the paint with a medium-to-hot iron.

7 Baste the square of polyester wadding to the wrong side of the painted silk square. Use several rows of basting to ensure the layers are held together securely.

8 Machine-quilt around some of the motifs or around all of them if you prefer.

9 Place the cushion backs with right sides together. Join them along one side with an 11.5 cm long seam at each end, leaving an opening in the middle for the zipper. Press the seam open. Sew the zipper into the opening and leave it open.

10 Place the cushion back and front together with right sides facing. Sew around the outside in a 1.5 cm seam. Trim the seams and turn the cushion to the right side through the zipper opening. Press lightly.

11 Stitch parallel rows around the cushion cover, stitching through all layers to make a 6 cm border all around.

12 Place the cushion insert inside the stencilled cover.

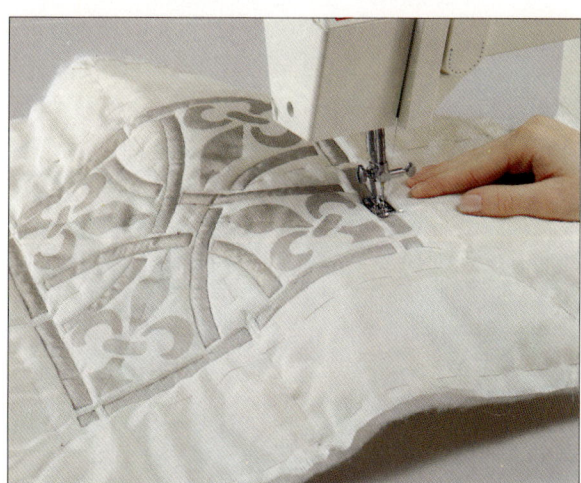

Far left: Lining up the stencil on the silk square
Above: Painting in the stencil design
Left: Quilting around the stencilled motifs

STENCILLED CURTAIN & TIE-BACK

A simple calico curtain takes on a new elegance with a padded and stencilled border and matching tie-back. The instructions given here are for making the border only. You will need to make up your own curtain when the border is attached.

Below: Painting in the stencil curtain design
Below right: Pinning the stencilled fabric over the interfacing
Far right: The completed curtain and tie-back

MATERIALS
sufficient calico
masking tape
firm interfacing (not iron-on)
tracing paper
pencil
sheets of clear acetate for the stencils
fineline permanent marker pen
sharp craft knife
newspaper
brown wrapping paper
fabric paint
old saucer or plate for a palette
stencil brush
piping (either readymade or make
　your own)
pelmet stiffening or very firm iron-on
　interfacing
pins
matching sewing thread
2 small brass rings

INSTRUCTIONS
See the design on the Pull Out Pattern Sheet.
1.5 cm seams allowed.

CURTAIN BORDER

1 Cut a piece of calico 25 cm wide and the length of the curtain. You will probably need to cut this down the length of the fabric so as to avoid any joins.

2 Trace the stencil design from the Pattern Sheet on to the acetate using the fineline pen. Cut out the stencil with the sharp knife.

3 Cover your work surface with newspaper with a sheet of brown wrapping paper on top. Tape the fabric strip to this work surface.

4 Position the stencil on one end of the strip, 4.5 cm from one long edge. Tape the stencil in place.

5 Pour a little of the fabric paint into the saucer. Load the stencil brush with a small amount of the paint and paint in the stencil design with a dabbing motion. Leave this section to dry before lifting the stencil and placing it on the next section to be

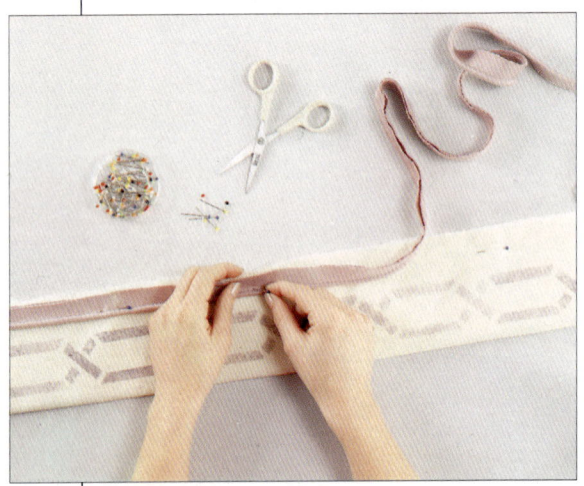

side of the curtain. Turn under the raw edge and slipstitch in place. Press well.

TIE-BACK

See the design on the Pull Out Pattern Sheet.

1 Cut two pieces of calico to the shape of the tie-back. Make the stencil in the same way as for the curtain border. Mark the outline of the tie-back and the halfway point.

2 Place the fabric and paint the stencil in the same way as for the curtain border, lifting the stencil (when the paint is dry) to paint in the second half, matching the pattern and the halfway points.

3 Cut the pelmet stiffening to the same shape as the tie-back. Remove the backing and press it on to the back of the stencilled calico. If using the iron-on interfacing, ignore the reference to the backing.

4 Trim away the excess calico, leaving a border 2 cm all around. Pin the piping to the calico with right sides facing and raw edges even. Clip the curves for ease. Stitch around the edge, close to the piping cord.

5 Remove the other backing and fold the seam allowance to the back. Clip the curves around the edge of the second piece of calico. Press the seam allowance to the wrong side. Place this piece on the back of the stencilled piece, with wrong sides together, and slipstitch into place. Press well. Sew a small brass ring to each end.

painted. When you reposition the stencil, take care to match the pattern exactly. Fix all the paint when it is dry.

6 Fold the fabric strip over double lengthways, with wrong sides together, placing a double thickness of interfacing in between. Pin the top layer of the calico and the interfacing together along the top edge.

7 Pin and stitch the piping to the top edge of the calico and the interfacing, with right sides together.

8 Pin the piped edge to the edge of your curtain, with right sides facing and raw edges even. Stitch close to the piping. Press the border out, folding the free edge to the wrong

Lacy bed linen (see page 22)

LACY BED LINEN

This is a delightful way to create the effect of exclusive lace-trimmed bed linen without the cost. All you need is a short length of lace which you can use to stencil the design on to pillowcases, sheets and quilt covers.

MATERIALS

plain sheet, pillowcase and quilt cover
length of lace, approximately 6 cm wide
narrow masking tape
newspaper
sheets of brown wrapping paper
pins
black fabric paint
water
mouth-spray diffuser
grey and peach satin ribbon, 1 cm and 1.5 cm wide
matching sewing thread

INSTRUCTIONS

1 Starting at one end of the wide hem at the top end of the sheet, pin the lace in place so that the decorative edge of the lace runs along the hemmed edge. Place a line of masking tape to cover the two short ends and the long straight edge of the lace.

2 Lay sheets of newspaper on your work surface to protect it from overspray. Lay brown paper on top of the newspaper to protect the bed linen from the dye in the newsprint.

3 Remove the pins from the lace and lay the section of sheet with the lace attached on to the brown paper. Cover all parts of the sheet, except for the lace section, with more brown paper, taping it in place.

4 In a small bottle, mix the black fabric paint with sufficient water to give a thin, very liquid consistency. Test the effect on a piece of scrap fabric, using the mouth-spray diffuser. Aim for a light-grey spotty texture that will spread through the holes in the lace on to the fabric. When you are confident with the colour and the diffuser, spray the lace-covered sheet in the same way. Leave to dry.

5 Move the length of lace along the sheet top, re-masking in the same way each time, until the whole length of the border is complete. Remove all the masking and leave the paint to dry for twenty-four hours.

6 Fix the paint using an iron set to the hottest setting appropriate for the sheet fabric.

Top: Pinning and taping the lace in place
Right: Spraying the paint over the lace

7 Pin and stitch a length of 1 cm wide peach ribbon and 1.5 cm grey ribbon parallel to the edge of the lace, turning in the raw edges at the ends.

8 To decorate the pillowcases and quilt cover, mask, pin and spray the lace in the same way up to the first corner. At the corner, stick masking tape across the lace at an angle of 45° to mitre the corner. To continue along the next side, match up the pattern in the lace, mitring again at the corner with masking tape. Continue in this way until the border on all four sides is complete. Sew on peach satin ribbon as for the sheet.

Top: Pinning the lengths of ribbon in place
Above: Mitre the corners on the pillowcases using masking tape

SPONGED CURTAINS

These simple floor-length curtains will add style to any modern living room and can be painted in any colour to complement your decor. The technique is so simple that even the children can paint a set of curtains for their own rooms.

MATERIALS
sufficient plain fabric
sheets of newspaper
masking tape
opaque black and white fabric
*   paints*
old saucer or plate for a palette
natural sponge

INSTRUCTIONS

1 Mask all around your work area with plenty of newspaper before you begin.

2 Tear sheets of newspaper into long irregularly shaped strips. Do not try to be too neat – the effect will be more dramatic if you allow a fair degree of variation.

3 Measure the area to be covered by the curtain. Your fabric will need to be twice the width of the window times the length to the floor, plus an allowance for hems and headings. Sew together enough fabric for your curtain but do not hem it or make the heading. Lay the fabric on the newspaper on the work area.

4 With masking tape, join together enough strips of newspaper to fit across the width of the fabric.

5 Leaving irregular gaps between the rows, stick the newspaper strips across the fabric, using little loops of masking tape to join the underside of the newspaper to the fabric. Cover the length of the fabric in this way, breaking up the rows with small 'islands' of paper as you move towards the top.

6 Pour some black paint on to the saucer or plate. Dip the damp sponge into the paint and, starting at the bottom, apply the paint between the rows of newspaper.

7 At the beginning of each new row, add a little white paint to the black, adding more white paint with each successive row so that the colour gradually lightens to grey as you work up the fabric. When you reach the top where you have the islands of paper, the colour should be quite light.

8 Allow the paint to dry before removing the strips of newspaper. Make the other curtain in the same way.

9 When the paint is dry, iron each piece of fabric on the wrong side to fix the colour. Finish making the curtains in the usual way.

Top left: Sticking irregularly shaped strips of newspaper aross the fabric
Centre left: Applying the paint with a sponge to the area between the paper strips
Bottom left: When the paint is dry, remove the strips of newspaper
Right: The completed curtains

Ornamental Painting

Painting your own designs on to kitchenware, glassware and ornaments will give your home a style that is quite unique. You will be able to turn inexpensive crockery from the supermarket into pieces you will be proud to display.

There are special paints available for decorating glass, ceramics, china and wood. Choose the right paint for the job and carefully follow the manufacturer's instructions. While the special ceramic and glass paints are relatively easy to use and are purpose-designed, they are not intended for items that will take a great deal of wear. Keep them for the more ornamental pieces.

More hardy are these painted terracotta pots which are definitely meant to be used. Paint the pots with simple designs of your own or isolate an element from any of the stencil designs given in this book. Stencilling a pot is quite simple as long as you take care to keep the stencil in contact with the pot and tape it in place while you work. You can make a very simple but effective design by masking off areas of the pot with masking tape and then sponging the exposed areas. Experiment with combinations of colours and designs to build up a collection of personalised pots like this to dress up a sunny corner. An oil-based mix of satin and gloss paints, or artists acrylic colours are both quite suitable for use on terracotta.

MEDITERRANEAN PLATTER

Bring all the
sunshine of the
Mediterranean into
your home with this
brightly coloured
platter. This method
of decorating is
called 'resist
painting' where a
material (in this
case the chinagraph
pencil) prevents the
paint from covering
a certain area. To
create this primitive
design, you will
need a mixture of
glass and ceramic
paints.

MATERIALS
plain white platter
glass paint, emerald green
ceramic paints in 4 colours of
    your choice
paintbrushes for applying the design
    and a larger one for the varnish
chinagraph pencil
soft dry cloth
mineral turpentine
ceramic varnish

*Right: Drawing
the design with a
chinagraph pencil*

Above: The completed platter
Right: Painting the design with ceramic paints

INSTRUCTIONS

1 Practise drawing the fish motif on a scrap of paper until you are happy with it, then, using the chinagraph pencil, draw the design on to the platter. Those areas that are covered with the chinagraph will remain white on the finished platter.

2 Carefully paint in the fish with the ceramic paints. Keep the colours bright with a strong contrast such as deep blue and yellow, purple and orange, or black and gold.

3 Paint the border pattern in another pair of bright colours such as red and blue. Don't try to be too neat. This primitive style lends itself quite well to a little irregularity.

4 Paint the water around the fish in emerald green glass paint, applying the paint in a wave pattern to indicate water and waves. Use glass paint for this part of the design as it is more translucent than ceramic paint.

5 When the paint is completely dry, rub off the chinagraph lines with the soft dry cloth to reveal the white china beneath.

6 If you need to tidy up the edges of the platter, use the soft cloth soaked in mineral turpentine.

7 To protect your platter, paint it with a coat of ceramic varnish.

Above: Cleaning off the chinagraph pencil
Right: Applying a coat of ceramic varnish

SOPHISTICATED GLASSES

MATERIALS
scrap paper
pencil
wine glasses
glass paint in the colours of
*   your choice*
fine paintbrush

INSTRUCTIONS

1 Before you begin painting, it is a good idea to plan your design on some scrap paper. Don't be too restricted by this plan, just use it to decide what works well and what doesn't.

2 Using the fine paintbrush, begin working from either the top or the bottom of the glass, painting a winding vine around the bowl and stem. To ensure that the paint does not smudge while you are working, allow one area to dry before beginning the next one.

Above right: The completed glasses
Below left and right: Painting in the design of the vines and leaves

PAINTED PLATES

What a very bright and happy image these clowns create when painted on to a set of wall plaques! They make the perfect decoration for a child's room. Birthday cards, gift wrapping, toys and children's picture books are all good sources of inspiration for a project like this one.

MATERIALS
white wall plates
tracing paper
pencil
chinagraph pencil
ceramic paints: black, cherry red,
    lavender, blue, orange, yellow
    and green
ceramic varnish

INSTRUCTIONS

1 Draw or trace your chosen design on to tracing paper, then copy it on to a plate using the chinagraph pencil.

2 Take into account the round shape of the plate when you are drawing your design. You can make the feet follow the edge or the hands appear to support the top edge, or have the clown doing a handstand. Whatever design you choose, always cover as much of the plate as possible.

3 Draw in the outline with a line of black ceramic paint, then paint in the main features, such as the clothes and hair. Colour the clothes very bright and busy, with plenty of spots, checks and patches.

4 Fill in the background with another busy pattern of circles, triangles or wavy lines painted in more bright contrasting colours.

5 Allow the paint to dry completely, then paint with a protective coat of ceramic varnish.

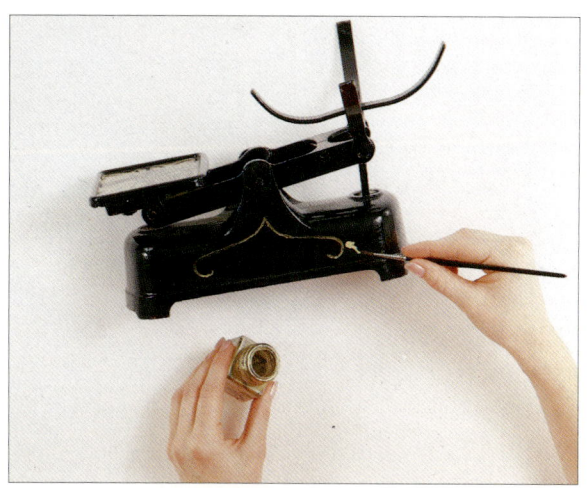

STRAWBERRY TRAY

What a charming notion! Decorate a simple pine tray with a pattern derived from your favourite china tea set. On the other hand, if you like this strawberry design, you can buy some china to match. Or you can use the techniques described here to paint a tray to match your own tea set.

Top: Tracing the design from the tea set
Above: Cutting out the stencil

MATERIALS
pine tray
tracing paper
pencil
masking tape
sheets of clear acetate for the stencils
coloured pencils in appropriate colours
fineline permanent marker pen
sharp craft knife
cutting board (optional)
sandpaper
lint-free cloth
acrylic paints in appropriate colours
  (quick-drying stencil paints are
    ideal)
small stencil brush
old saucer or plate for a palette
clear varnish
5 cm paintbrush

INSTRUCTIONS

1 Tape small pieces of tracing paper over the areas of the design you wish to use. Trace off the elements either singly, as single leaves and strawberries, or as groups.

2 Using your tracings, combine the elements into a pleasing design. Trace the new outline on to another sheet of tracing paper. It is a good idea at this stage to colour in your design with the coloured pencils so you can judge its effectiveness.

3 Transfer the design to several sheets of acetate (one for each colour), using the fineline pen.

4 You will need to make a separate stencil for each colour. To do this, cut out of each sheet the elements you wish to paint in a particular colour, using the craft knife. Take care when

cutting out to leave 'bridges' in the design such as down the spine of a leaf or between stalks and leaves.

5 Sand the tray all over with the sandpaper until it is quite smooth. Wipe away the sandings with the lint-free cloth.

6 Position the first stencil (in this case the green one) on a corner of the tray and tape it in place. Place a small amount of paint on the saucer or plate. Using the small stencil brush, paint in the green areas of the design using a dabbing motion. Take care not to load the brush with too much paint. Repeat the process for all the green areas on the tray. Allow the paint to dry completely.

7 With the clean stencil brush, paint in the next colour (red) in the same way as the green, then the white and finally the yellow. To avoid smudging, make sure each last colour is dry before you apply the next one.

8 To complete the tray, you can decorate around the sides and around the handles with small stencils.

9 When all the stencilling is complete and the paint is dry, apply a coat of clear varnish to all the surfaces.

Below: Painting the first colour
Bottom: Completing the painting of the stencil

FOLK ART SHELF

———— ✳ ————

This delightful little shelf, destined to house a collection of thimbles, has been painted with a number of traditional folk art motifs relating to sewing and quilting. It is an original design by Annette Johnson. Craft shops sell shelves like this in a raw form, in a kit, or assembled ready to paint.

MATERIALS
small timber shelf
fineline permanent marker pen
blue saral paper
stylus
kneadable eraser
burnt umber oil paint
antiquing liquid
lint-free cloth
round sable brush, size 2
flat brushes, sizes 4 and 6
pale cream and dusty blue paint for base coats
Deco Art Americana paints: French grey blue, snow white, uniform blue, cranberry wine, burnt umber, avocado, ebony black, blue haze, raw sienna, light cinnamon, dusty rose, lavender, neutral grey, slate grey. (You can use any folk art paints in similar colours that are suitable for painting on wood.)
spray gloss varnish
wet and dry sandpaper, 600 grade
normal sandpaper

INSTRUCTIONS
See the designs on the Pull Out Pattern Sheet.

PREPARATION

1 Base coat the shelf with four coats of pale cream, sanding well between each coat. Do not sand the final coat.

2 Trace the painting designs and transfer them to the positions shown on the shelf, using the stylus and blue saral paper. Blue saral paper is not as waxy as graphite paper and will not clog the nib of your pen as you draw over the design lines.

3 Outline all the tracing lines using the fineline pen. If you make a mistake, wet a small piece of the wet and dry sandpaper and gently rub the mistake away.

4 Let the ink dry for about one hour then remove all visible saral lines with the kneadable eraser.

PAINTING

1 This shelf is painted using washes, i.e. a mix of 80% water and 20% paint. Use the round brush, size 2 for this step. When all the washes have been completed, shade with the flat brush that fits best in the area you are shading. Shading is done with full-strength paint and only the water in your brush.

2 Mix French grey blue and snow white. Wash all hearts, dots and commas dividing each drawing, the ribbon on the one bonnet, the scissor handles, the fabric on the quilt, the ruching on the dress, the band on the dress collar, two buttons, the bow on the straw hat, two pin heads, the bottom half of the fan, and the lettering. Shade in uniform blue.

3 Mix cranberry wine and burnt umber. Wash the button, all the flowers, stripes on the large button, and the quilt fabric. Shade with the same mixture.

4 Mix avocado, ebony black and snow white. Wash all the leaves and quilt fabric. Shade with a mixture of avocado and blue haze.

5 With blue haze, wash the dilly bag and the feather on the pen. Shade with blue haze.

6 With raw sienna, wash the letter next to the pen, the straw hat, the pin box, the button, the ruler, the thimble, the calendar, the quilt fabric, the nib of the pen, and the ink label. Shade with light cinnamon.

7 With light cinnamon, wash the pen handle, the umbrella handle, the cotton spool ends, the boot heel and sole. Shade with burnt umber.

8 With dusty rose, wash the umbrella frills, the top section of the fan, the button, the quilt, the scallop part of the boot, the bow on the dilly bag. Shade with burnt umber.

9 Mix lavender and neutral grey. Wash the cotton on the spool, the quilt, a button, the bow on the fan, the pins, the umbrella and bows, the quilt edge. Shade with the same mix.

10 With uniform blue, wash the ink bottle and the back part of the boot. Shade with uniform blue.

11 With snow white, wash the dress and bonnet. Shade with slate grey. With slate grey, wash the scissor blades. Shade with ebony black. When all the painting is dry, reinforce with the fineline pen any lines painted over. Paint the shelf edges with a 1:1 mixture of cream and dusty blue.

12 Varnish the shelf all over when the paint is dry.

Give your shelf an antique finish before varnishing, if you wish.

Furniture Facelifts

Decorative painting can work miracles on furniture that has become a little 'tired' and worn. Whether you have a garage full of well-used chairs or are a devotee of jumble sales, consider the possibilities that painting opens up.

Before you begin, make sure that the piece of furniture is worth all your hard work. Check that the structure is basically sound – or that you can fix any problems without undue cost. Remember, rotting timber will not be made stronger with a lovely stencilled pattern.

Next, prepare your surface well. If it is already painted, you will need to remove the old paint layers with a good paint stripper. Fill any holes and sand the entire piece until it is quite smooth. If it is not painted, you should still make sure the surface is clean and free of wax or polish and that there are no holes or cracks.

Which style of painting you choose is up to you. Stencilling lends itself very well to furniture and it is remarkably simple to achieve a very good result. Freehand painting requires a little more effort but the results are very rewarding.

The charming cane chair opposite was quite solid but very drab until its facelift. First it was sprayed with a white aerosol paint, using three light coats to give a good covering. The roses were first drawn on with a soft pencil and then painted with acrylic paints. You will need to mix colours to get this range of shades, using the darker ones to give depth to the design and the lighter ones for highlights.

TOY CHEST

A battered pine chest can take on a new lease of life with this wonderful painted design of friendly animals. As a special touch, personalise your painted chest with the name of the owner. If you want to hand it down from generation to generation, paint in the family name and you have the makings of a family heirloom which will be loved by generations of children.

MATERIALS

pine chest
steel wool
mineral turpentine (white spirit)
sandpaper
soapy water
rag
tracing paper
pencil
transfer paper
stylus
black fineline permanent marker pen
masking tape
acrylic paints in suitable colours,
    including black and white
old saucer or plate for a palette
suitable paintbrushes
clear gloss varnish

Below: Transferring the design to the toy chest
Below right: Painting in the design
Right: The completed toy chest

INSTRUCTIONS

See the design on the Pull Out Pattern Sheet.

1 The surface of the chest should be absolutely clean if the paint is to adhere properly. If there is any wax on the wood, remove it by rubbing with the steel wool dipped in mineral turpentine (white spirit). Wipe off all the grime and rubbings with the rag dipped in soapy water.

2 When the wood is quite dry sand the chest all over, inside and out.

3 Trace the design from the Pattern Sheet on to tracing paper. You will need to adjust the size of the design to suit the size of your own toy chest. The simplest way to do this is on a photocopying machine. Using two elements of the design, say the smallest and the biggest, work out an appropriate enlargement to suit you. If you do not have access to a photo-copier, use the grid method described on page 7 to enlarge the design.

4 When you have a drawing of the right size, tape it in position on the toy chest, using masking tape. Slip a sheet of transfer paper between the drawing and the wooden surface and go over all the outlines with the stylus, transferring them to the chest. On a wooden surface these markings may be quite faint so you will need to go over them with the pencil or the fineline pen.

5 Draw in the name in the space provided.

6 Using the old saucer or plate for your palette, mix up some paints with a little black or white to add tonal variation to the flat colours. Paint in the designs.

7 When the paint is completely dry, strengthen the outlines, whiskers and facial features by drawing over them with the fineline pen.

8 Paint one or two coats of clear gloss varnish over the whole chest to protect the painted design. You will also see how the colours come to life with a coat or two of varnish.

SPONGED CABINET

Transform an old cabinet, long past its prime, with a wonderful painted effect and new china handles painted to match. Before you begin working on your transformation, make sure that the cabinet is solid – don't waste your efforts on furniture that is about to fall apart.

MATERIALS

an old cabinet
newspaper
paint stripper
scraping tool
detergent
wood filler
sandpaper
wood primer
undercoat
5 cm paintbrush
water-based base colour (light colour)
water-based second colour (medium colour)
water-based third colour (darkest colour)
ceramic paint for the handles
natural sponge
plain white china handles
fine paintbrush

INSTRUCTIONS

1 You will first need to remove the old finish and for this step it is important to work in a well-ventilated room. Remove the old handles and spread plenty of newspaper on the floor. Use the paint stripper following the manufacturer's instructions.

2 Wash down the cabinet with a mild detergent-and-water solution. Fill any holes with wood filler.

3 When the cabinet is dry, sand it all over until it is quite smooth.

4 Apply a wood primer and then an undercoat, following the manufacturer's instructions. Allow the surface to dry between coats.

5 Apply the base coat (light colour) with the 5 cm paintbrush and allow it to dry.

6 Wet the sponge and squeeze out any excess water, leaving it just damp. Dip the sponge into the second paint colour, dabbing any excess paint off on some scrap paper. Dab the paint on. Do not cover the surface with this colour but leave plenty of gaps for the third colour.

7 After cleaning the sponge, apply the third colour in the same way, filling in the gaps and overlapping the sponging already in place.

8 While the cabinet is drying, you can decorate the new china handles with the ceramic paint and the fine paintbrush. Choose any design, such as flowers, leaves or ribbon garlands. If you need inspiration, china patterns on plates and cups are a good source of designs.

Right: Removing the old finish

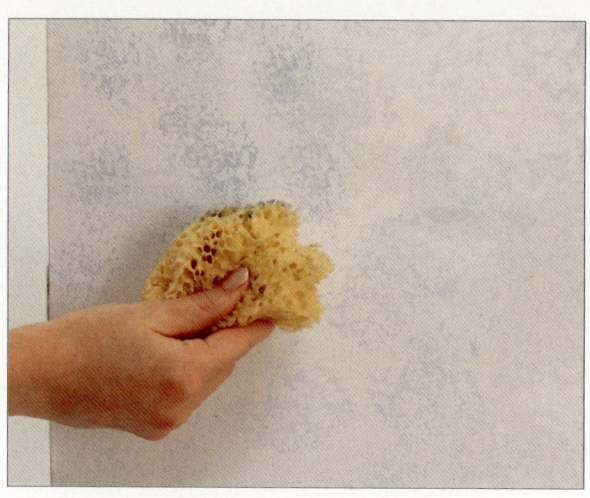

Top: Sponging on the third colour
Above: Painting the new china handles
Right: The completed cabinet

MARBLED PLANT STAND

A good marbling effect can be quite difficult to achieve so it is a good idea to practise on a spare piece of timber until you are happy with the result.

MATERIALS
plain wooden pedestal
wood for practising on
primer and/or undercoat
*black matt or low-sheen premium
  paint*
*white matt or low-sheen premium
  paint*
scumble medium
mineral turpentine
*paintbrushes, one small round, one
  6-8 cm and one fine artist's brush*
soft cloth
stipple brush
clear varnish
brush for applying varnish

INSTRUCTIONS

1 Apply primer and/or undercoat following the manufacturer's instructions.

2 Paint the pedestal with the black matt or low-sheen premium paint. Allow to dry.

3 Mix a white glaze consisting of 20% white matt or low-sheen premium paint, 20% mineral turpentine and 60% scumble medium. Dab on this white glaze, using the 6-8 cm brush. Don't completely white out the black background, but allow some of it to show through.

4 While the white glaze is still wet, dab over it with the soft cloth, crumpled. This should soften any hard edges and spread the white glaze.

5 Continue to soften the glaze by working over it with a stipple brush and the soft cloth dipped in mineral turpentine.

6 Mix a little black glaze using the same proportions of paint, scumble medium and mineral turpentine as for the white glaze. Using this and the fine paintbrush, draw in some veins. Make them quite irregular and broken and soften any hard edges with the stipple brush.

7 Using the white glaze and the fine paintbrush, draw in some white veins and stipple as before.

8 When the paint is dry, apply a coat or two of clear varnish to give the glossy appearance of marble.

Above right: Painting the pedestal
Right: Applying the white glaze

Top: Dabbing off some of the white glaze
Above: Painting in the veins
Right: The marbled plant stand

STENCILLED BEDROOM

Transform a dull room into a little girl's delight with some very inexpensive touches. The stencilled bluebirds and trailing bows are repeated on the walls, bed, chest of drawers and even give new life to an old cane chair.

If you are really enthusiastic, you can stencil some bed linen and even floorboards in the same bluebird theme.

The same design has been used for all the stencilling, with adaptations to the basic design to suit the particular angle or surface where it is to be used. For example, the stencilled border that travels up the wall to the old chimney breast uses only the right-hand bird from the original design, with the upper wing omitted.

BED DRAPES

Add a touch of romance with these simple bed drapes, highlighted with bows and stencilling.

MATERIALS

water-based paint in white and sky blue
large brush
damp cotton cloth
electric drill
3 wall plugs
3 brass hooks
approximately 16 m white muslin
5 m of 2 cm wide peach satin ribbon
masking tape
white sewing thread
tracing paper
pencil
sheets of clear acetate for the stencil
fineline permanent marker pen
sharp craft knife
old saucer or plate for a palette
quick-drying stencil paints or acrylic paint in blue and peach
stencil brush

INSTRUCTIONS

See the design on the Pull Out Pattern Sheet.

1 Paint the wall with the white water-based paint. Allow to dry. Mix up a pale blue wash by diluting the sky blue water-based paint. Using the large brush, swish on the pale blue to give a soft streaky effect. If some parts are too strong, lighten them by lifting a little of the colour with the damp cloth while the paint is still wet. Allow the paint to dry thoroughly.

2 Find the centre point on the wall approximately 1.5 m above the bed. Drill and plug a hole at this point, then screw in a small brass hook.

3 Find the centre of the 16 m length of muslin. Gather the fabric gently at the centre and tie a bow of satin ribbon to hold the gathering in place. Leave the ends of the ribbon to trail down. Tie a second bow to the hook and then around the muslin to create a double bow with four trailing ends. Trim the ends at various lengths, cutting them at an angle.

4 Mark a point on either side of the bed, approximately 30 cm below the centre hook. Experiment to find the right point by gathering and draping the muslin. Drill and plug a hole at each of these points and insert the brass hooks.

Above right: Securing the muslin drape
Right: Stencilling the bluebird design

Left: The bed drapes

5 On the muslin, mark equal
distances on either side of the
centre where the drape finishes. As
before, tie two satin bows at each of
these points, attaching the muslin to
the hooks. Remove the tape.

6 Hem the muslin at an appropriate
point. You can have it ending just
above floor level or have it mounded
up luxuriously as shown on page 50.

7 Trace the individual bluebirds
from the Pattern Sheet on to a
sheet of acetate with the fineline pen.
Cut out the stencil with the craft knife.
Tape each one to the wall above the
centre hook. Place a little paint on the
old saucer or plate. Remove the
muslin before you begin painting.
Paint in the stencil design. Clean the
stencils in water several times while
you work as they become clogged
very easily.

8 Make a separate stencil for the
bow in the same way as for the
bluebirds. Stencil the three birds with
trailing ribbons around each of the
side hooks and one more bluebird
below each hook as shown. Always
make sure the paint is dry when lifting
and moving stencils to their next
position.

9 When all the paint is dry, replace
the muslin drape.

CANE CHAIR

This lovely old Lloyd Loom chair has been stencilled with bluebirds, but the wall stencil would have been too delicate for the texture of the chair so a stencil with more dramatic effect has been chosen.

Below: The completed cane chair
Right: Spraying the first stencil
Below right: Adding the second colour

MATERIALS
white cane chair
spray paint in white, blue and peach
tracing paper
pencil
3 sheets of clear acetate for the stencils
fineline permanent marker pen
sharp craft knife
paper for masking
masking tape

INSTRUCTIONS
See the design on the Pull Out Pattern Sheet.

1 First spray the chair all over with blue. Allow to dry. Do not attempt to cover the white background completely.

2 Trace the three stencil designs from the Pattern Sheet on to three pieces of acetate with the fineline pen. Cut out the stencils.

3 Tape the bow stencil on the centre back of the chair. Tape paper around the stencil to mask the rest of the chair. Spray the stencil in a peach colour. It is best to spray several light coats from about 30 cm away until the cane is well covered but not clogged with paint.

4 Tape one bluebird stencil on the left-hand side of the bow. Mask around it as before. Spray the stencil in white as for the bow. When the paint is dry, carefully remove the stencil. Paint the bluebird on the other side in the same way.

CHEST OF DRAWERS

MATERIALS
chest of drawers
tracing paper
pencil
sheets of clear acetate for the stencils
fineline permanent marker pen
sharp craft knife
paper for masking
masking tape
old saucer or plate for a palette
fast-drying stencil paints or acrylic
    paints in blue and peach
clear varnish

INSTRUCTIONS
See the designs on the Pull Out
Pattern Sheet.

1 If your chest of drawers is looking
a little battered, you will need to
give it a couple of coats of white,
water-based gloss paint before you
begin stencilling.

2 Trace the large bow from the
Pattern Sheet on to a piece of
acetate, using the fineline pen. For the
smaller bow, trace the design from the
Pattern Sheet on to tracing paper.
Sketch in another loop on the left-
hand side of the bow. Turn this bow

slightly so the ribbon tails hang vertically. Transfer the design to another
piece of acetate, using the fineline
pen. Mark in the position of the
bluebirds on both sides so you can
align them properly when you come
to paint them in. Cut out the stencils
using the craft knife. Make a bird
stencil in the same way. If you have
already made a stencil of which you
could use a part, simply mask off any
area you do not wish to use.

3 Mark the centre of each drawer.
Place a little paint in the old
saucer or plate. Position and paint the
stencils as shown in the photograph,
cleaning and flipping over the stencils
as necessary. Take care not to lift and
move the stencils until the paint is
completely dry to avoid smudging.

4 When all the stencilling is
complete, paint the chest with a
coat of clear varnish.

*This is another
well-used piece of
furniture that has
been given a new
lease of life. You
will need to adapt
the stencil used
for the bed drapes
for the smaller bow
on the second
drawer. The larger
bow is given on the
Pattern Sheet and
the bluebird is the
one on the right
above the bed
drapes.*

*Below left: Cutting out the
stencils
Below: Painting the stencil
on the drawers*

WALL BORDER

A dainty border is a pretty feature on most walls and especially those where there are interesting nooks and crannies to be emphasised. Border stencils, such as this one, look most effective along skirting boards, dado rails, below window ledges or along cornices.

MATERIALS
pencil
ruler
sheets of clear acetate for the stencils
fineline permanent marker pen
sharp craft knife
masking tape
old saucer or plate for a palette
fast-drying stencil paint or acrylic
    paint in peach, terracotta and blue
stencil brush

INSTRUCTIONS
See the design on the Pull Out Pattern Sheet.

1 Trace the bluebirds from the Pattern Sheet on to the acetate with the fineline pen. Trace part of the peach bows, using a dotted line, to help you position the design later on. Mark the top and side lines to use as registration marks for lining up your design accurately. Cut out the bluebird stencil with the sharp knife. Make a separate stencil for the bows in the same way, marking the top and sides as before.

2 Rule a faint horizontal line in pencil on the wall where you wish the top of the stencil to fall. Line up the top mark on the stencil with the pencil line on the wall. Tape the stencil in place. Place a small amount of peach paint on the saucer. Paint in the peach bows with a dabbing motion. Leave to dry.

3 Lift off the bow stencil and tape it in the next position, using the registration marks you have drawn. Continue until you have finished the entire border of bows. Clean your stencil frequently to avoid it becoming clogged with paint.

4 When the paint is nearly dry, dab on some terracotta colour with a clean brush at the points where the ribbons twist and overlap to give a three-dimensional effect.

5 Work along the border with the bluebird stencil and blue paint in the same way as for the bows, matching registration marks and the dotted lines. Clean the stencil frequently as you work.

Left: Use the wall border to accentuate interesting corners

RIBBON BOWS

MATERIALS
sheet of clear acetate for the stencil
fineline permanent marker pen
sharp craft knife
pencil
masking tape
old saucer or plate for a palette
fast-drying stencil paint or acrylic
  paint in peach and terracotta
stencil brush

INSTRUCTIONS
See the design on the Pull Out Pattern Sheet.

1 Trace the stencil design from the Pattern Sheet on to the acetate with the fineline pen. Cut it out.

2 Mark on the wall the position of the top of the picture. Remove the picture. Tape the stencil, centred above the picture, so that the ends of the bow trail down behind it.

3 Place a little peach paint in the saucer. Paint in the design.

4 When the paint is nearly dry, dab on some terracotta colour with a clean brush. Do this where the

ribbons twist and overlap to give a three-dimensional effect. Blend the terracotta colour into the peach so there are no sudden colour changes.

Above: The ribbon bow
Left: Stencilling the peach colour

FLORENTINE HALLWAY

This is an ideal situation for a stencilled 'wallpaper' effect. Paint the wall below the dado rail in a colour to complement the stencilling.

WALL PATTERN

MATERIALS
long ruler
pencil
sheets of clear acetate for the stencils
fineline permanent marker pen
sharp craft knife
string and weight for a plumb line
masking tape
old saucer or plate for a palette
fast-drying stencil paint
stencil brush

INSTRUCTIONS

1 Work out how far apart you wish to have the motifs – approximately 9 cm apart vertically and 7.5 cm apart horizontally looks good. For tight corners, you will need only one or two motifs on the stencil, but it will obviously speed up your work in the larger areas to have six or eight motifs on the stencil. Consider cutting two stencils – a small and a large one.

2 Trace the motif from this page on to the acetate with the fineline pen. Draw in horizontal and vertical registration lines to help you align the stencils. Draw in with dotted lines the other motif outlines. Cut out the stencils with the craft knife.

3 Find the centre of the wall and, using the plumb line and a long ruler, lightly mark a vertical pencil line from the ceiling down to the dado rail.

4 Tape the stencil to the wall with masking tape, lining up the first vertical row of motifs with the pencil line on the wall and placing the first motif about 5 cm from the ceiling. Check that this gives you sufficient room (approximately 12 cm) above the dado rail for the border. You may need to adjust the spacing slightly.

5 Place a little paint in the saucer or plate and begin painting in the stencil with a dabbing motion to give a soft grainy texture. If you are using a small two-motif stencil, overlap the lower one you have just painted with the upper one on the next section to space the rows correctly.

6 When the paint is dry, work the next vertical row of stencils, matching up the dotted lines with the painted motifs. Continue stencilling, adjusting the spacing slightly to allow for awkward corners or uneven rows. Stencil up to 13 cm of the mirror's edge. If there are any large gaps near the curved surface, it is best to leave these until you have painted the border and then add in another motif where necessary.

Right: Cutting out the stencil
Far right: The stencilled hallway and table

Follow these steps to ensure that the border follows exactly the curve of the mirror or table.

HALL TABLE

MATERIALS
tracing paper
large sheet of white paper
pencil
sheets of clear acetate for the stencils
fineline permanent marker pen
scissors
sharp craft knife
masking tape
old saucer or plate for a palette
fast-drying stencil paints or acrylic
*   paints in white and blue*
stencil brush
kitchen paper
clear varnish

Above right: Cutting the curved tracings
Right: Stencilling in the first colour on the table

INSTRUCTIONS
See the design on the Pull Out Pattern Sheet.

1 Trace the exact curve of the table on to the large sheet of white paper.

2 Trace the design from the Pattern Sheet on to sheets of tracing paper. Cut slits alternately in the top and bottom of these tracings so that they can bend. Tape the border design over the curved traced line on the white paper, bending it to fit.

3 Lay the acetate over the top of the design on the curved line and trace in the adapted design with the fineline pen, extending and shortening lines as necessary. Cut one stencil for each colour to be used, based on this adapted design. Mark dotted registration lines and the curved line of the table's edge on both stencils.

4 Tape the 'white' stencil in place and dab in the white paint to make a soft grainy effect. Leave to dry before removing the stencil.

5 Tape the 'blue' stencil in place, matching dotted lines and registration marks. Dab in the blue colour, using very little paint on an almost dry brush (remove excess paint with the kitchen paper) to give the subtle mottled finish. Leave to dry before removing the stencil.

6 Paint the table top with a coat of clear varnish.

MIRROR BORDER

1 Trace the design from the Pattern Sheet on to the acetate with the fineline pen. Cut the bottom edge of the stencil so it will run along the dado rail and make the stencilling job much easier. Tape the stencil in place and paint as for the table border.

2 When you reach a corner, lay a piece of masking tape across the corner at 45° to mitre the corner. Paint up to the tape on both stencils.

3 Make a curved stencil in the same way as for the table top. Paint in the curved mirror frame in the same way and then paint in the straight sides, mitring the corners at the bottom to match up with the rest of the border.

Top: The mirror border
Above: Stencilling in the second colour on the table

STENCILLED BATHROOM

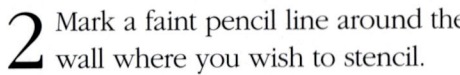

Is your bathroom quite functional but a bit drab? This wall stencil can be reduced to one-fifth of its size to decorate a pile of fluffy towels or the pretty flounce around the washbasin.

WALL BORDER

MATERIALS

water-based interior house paints in white and yellow
brush or roller
damp natural sponge
pencil
ruler
old plates or saucers for palettes
sheets of clear acetate for the stencils
fineline permanent marker pen
sharp craft knife
cutting board (optional)
masking tape
fast-drying stencil paints or acrylic paints in yellow, dark pink and green
small sponges

INSTRUCTIONS

See the stencil design on the Pull Out Pattern Sheet.

1 Paint the walls white and then, using the large damp sponge dipped in the yellow interior paint, dab paint on to the wall in an even manner. Take care not to have too much paint on the sponge.

2 Mark a faint pencil line around the wall where you wish to stencil.

3 Make two stencils – one for the flowers and one for the leaves. Trace the flowers from the Pattern Sheet on to one sheet of acetate with the fineline pen, drawing in the leaves with dotted lines. Cut out the flowers. Make a second stencil for the leaves, marking in the flowers with dotted lines. Cut out the leaves.

4 Tape the flower stencil in position on the pencil line. Using a small sponge and the yellow stencil paint, dab in the colour around the outside of the flowers. Dab in the pink colour at the flower centres, blending the pink with the yellow. Stencil the flowers all around the wall in this way, linking the stencils by matching up the dotted lines.

5 In the saucers or plates, mix up several shades of green, from lime to emerald, by combining the yellow and green acrylic paints in different proportions. Tape the leaf stencil in place at the first position, matching the dotted lines to the flower outlines. Dab in the green, varying the shades of green over the design to add interest. Apply the colour lightly to blend in with the sponged effect on the wall.

Left: Sponging the walls with yellow
Above right: The stencilled bathroom
Right: Stencilling in the first colour
Far right: Stencilling in the second colour

To set off your stylish new bathroom, trim a set of towels with a stencilled fabric strip to match the walls. Highlight the colours of the stencilling with bands of satin ribbon.

TOWEL

MATERIALS

towel

strip of smooth white cotton fabric, approximately 20 cm wide x width of the towel

pencil

ruler

sheets of clear acetate for the stencils

fineline permanent marker pen

sharp craft knife

cutting board (optional)

masking tape

paper or fabric for masking

fabric paints in yellow, dark pink and green

old plate or saucer for a palette

stencil brush

satin ribbon in two colours, twice as long as the towel is wide plus 4 cm

matching sewing thread

INSTRUCTIONS

See the designs on the Pull Out Pattern Sheet.

Right: The stencilled towels and bathmat, made in the same way as the towels, using the larger stencil

1 Make two stencils – one for the flowers and one for the leaves. Trace the flowers from the Pattern Sheet, drawing in the leaves with dotted lines. Draw in a horizontal line at the top and bottom for registration lines. Cut out the flowers. Make a stencil in the same way for the leaves, drawing in the flowers with dotted lines.

2 Mask your work area with paper or fabric. Tape the cotton fabric strip to the masking.

3 With the ruler and pencil, draw in a faint horizontal line 5 cm from the top edge to match up with the line on the stencil.

4 Tape the leaves stencil on top of the fabric strip, matching lines. Paint in the leaves in a mixture of yellow and green. Allow the paint to dry before lifting the stencil and taping it in its new position, matching dotted lines and registration marks. Complete the border of leaves in this way.

5 Using the flower stencil and working in the same way as for the leaves, paint the outside of the flowers in yellow. For the flower centres, blend in dark pink paint. Allow to dry. Fix the paints following the manufacturer's instructions.

6 Trim the stencilled strip along the pencil lines. Stitch the stencilled strip along the width of the towel, turning under the raw edges at both ends and stitching them down.

7 Pin a length of satin ribbon over the raw edges of the fabric strip and stitch it in place. Stitch another length of ribbon parallel to the first.